Chipper the CHEETAH

Come on a great adventure with me and learn all about my family

TRUE TO LIFE BOOKS

Educating children about endangered species

by Jan Latta

Hello! My name is Chipper and I am a cheetah.
I live in the open grass lands of Africa
with my brothers and sisters.

Cheetahs first appeared on Earth over four million years ago. We once lived in North America, Europe, Africa and Asia.

Now we are found only in Africa
and sometimes in Asia.

Our bodies are covered in spots – except for our throats, bellies and tails. Sometimes people mistake us for leopards.

We're the only animals to have black lines running from eyes to mouth. They help to lessen the glare from the sun.

Cheetahs are built for speed. We have special paws and claws to grip the ground. Our nose, lungs, heart, liver and blood vessels are larger than normal.

Our bodies are streamlined and our spine is like a spring. Our tail helps us keep our balance when we change directions.

Cheetahs are the fastest animal on land.
We can sprint up to 115 kilometres
over a short distance.

We can cover seven to eight metres in one stride and zoom from zero to 45 kilometres in just two seconds. But we get tired after 100 metres.

My mum gave birth to three cubs. They are born blind but start to see after four to ten days. They feed entirely on mum's milk for six weeks. Then, they learn to hunt.

We go to the highest ground to search for prey on the plains. We climb trees to get a better view.

We hide in the grass waiting for our chance to creep up close to our prey. Then with a burst of great speed we start the chase.

Cheetahs are carnivores, which means we eat meat. Mum teaches us how to hunt for food. She watches over us while we eat, protecting us from other animals.

Keeping clean is a daily activity.
We groom others and ourselves using our rough tongues, just like house cats.

We use lots of sounds to communicate. We hiss, chirp, growl, bark, yelp, bleat and purr very loudly. But we never roar!

Fewer than 12,500 cheetahs are left in the world. We are losing our habitat and the animals we depend on for food.

Some of us are killed as pests or poached for our beautiful coats. Every day is a struggle to survive. Without help, we cannot outrun extinction.

CHEETAH FACTS

SCIENTIFIC NAME
Acinonyx jubatus.
(Cheetahs are further classified into five African subspecies and two Asian subspecies.)

HABITAT
Cheetahs are found in several countries in Africa and in Iran. They range primarily across temperate grasslands and tropical savannahs, but can also be found in thick vegetation and mountainous areas.

WEIGHT
36 to 65 kilos, with males slightly larger and heavier than females.

LENGTH
1.8 to 2.15 metres.

AT BIRTH
- Cheetahs weigh 250-300 grams at birth, but develop quickly.
- Cubs are born blind and begin to see after 4-10 days.
- Cubs depend on mothers' milk for the first 4-6 weeks.

DIET
Cheetahs are mainly meat eaters. They like small antelope, including impala and gazelle, warthog, game birds and hare. When food is scarce, they will eat birds' eggs and fruit.

PREDATORS
Mainly humans through habitat destruction and hunting. Also lions, leopards and hyenas may kill the young.

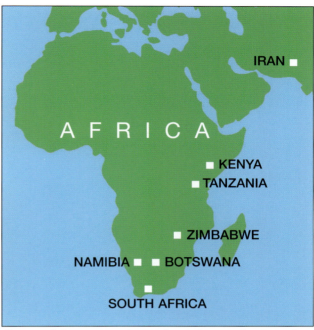

Some of the areas where cheetahs can be found

LIFE SPAN
Around 7 years in the wild; 8-12 years in captivity. High infant mortality rate.

NUMBERS REMAINING (estimate)
Fewer than 12,500.

DID YOU KNOW?
- As long as 3,000 years ago, humans kept cheetahs as symbols of royalty and for hunting.
- Cheetahs have been recorded at 95 kilometers per hour.
- Cheetahs are so tired after capturing prey they rest for 30 minutes before eating.
- A very small number of cheetahs have black stripes and big blotchy spots. They are called King cheetahs.
- Namibia has the largest population of wild cheetahs, about 2,500.
- Cheetahs run on their toes. At full speed there are times when their feet don't touch the ground.

An amazing moment for photographer Jan Latta when two cheetahs came up to her in Kenya.

SUGGESTED READING

CHEETAH
Taylor Morrison, 1998.

CHEETAHS
(Nature Watch Series)
Diane M. MacMillan, 1998.

CHEETAHS (Animals in Danger)
Rod Theodorou, 2001.

CHEETAHS (Zoo Books)
Linda C. Wood, J. Bonrett, et al, 2000.

CHEETAHS
Luke Hunter, 2000.

CHEETAHS (Endangered)
Shona Grimby, 1999.

CHEETAHS: BIG CATS (Naturebooks)
Jenny Markert, 2001.

CHEETAHS FOR KIDS (Wildlife for Kids Series)
Winnie MacPherson, 1998.

THE CHEETAH (Animal Close-ups)
Philippe Dupont, Valerie Tracqui, 1992.

THE CHEETAH
(Endangered Animals & Habitats Series)
Nathan Aaseng, 2000.

INTERESTING WEBSITES

CHEETAH CONSERVATION FUND
www.cheetah.org

CHEETAH OUTREACH
www.cheetah.co.za

DE WILDT CHEETAH AND WILDLIFE CENTRE
www.dewildt.org.za

KID'S PLANET
www.kidsplanet.org

NATIONAL GEOGRAPHIC
www.nationalgeographic.com/kids

SAN DIEGO ZOO
www.sandiegozoo.org

THE BIG ZOO
www.thebigzoo.com

THE CHEETAH SPOT
www.cheetahspot.com

THE SMITHSONIAN NATIONAL ZOO
http://nationalzoo.si.edu

WILD ABOUT CATS
www.wildaboutcats.org

WORLD WIDE FUND
CONSERVATION ORGANISATION
www.panda.org/

WORLD WILDLIFE FUND
www.worldwildlife.org/